easynoodles

First published in the USA in 2003
Ryland Peters & Small, Inc.
519 Broadway, 5th Floor
New York, NY 10012
www.rylandpeters.com

10 9 8 7 6 5 4 3 2 1

Library of Congress Cataloging-in-Publication Data

Barber, Kimiko.

Easy noodles : recipes from China, Japan, and
Southeast Asia / Kimiko Barber ; photography by
William Lingwood.

    p. cm.

Includes index.

ISBN 1-84173-386-X

1. Cookery (Pasta) 2. Cookery, Asian. I. Title.

TX809.M17 B355 2003

641.8'2--dc21

                          2002152847

Printed in China

Designer Luis Peral-Aranda
Commissioning Editor Elsa Petersen-Schepelern
Editors Katherine Steer, Helen Martineau
Production Deborah Wehner
Art Director Gabriella Le Grazie
Publishing Director Alison Starling

Food Stylist Joss Herd
Stylist Liz Belton

Notes

All spoon measurements are level unless
otherwise specified.

Uncooked or partly cooked eggs should not be
served to the very young, the very old or frail, or
to pregnant women.

Most of the ingredients used in this book are
available in larger supermarkets. For other
ingredients, visit Asian markets, Chinese,
Japanese, or Southeast Asian stores. Others are
available via mail order or online.

contents

oodles of noodles ...

Noodles are the "fast food" of Asia—they are quick, instantly satisfying, healthy, and wholesome to eat. It is because the Asian noodles are made from many different varieties of starch—unlike Italian pasta, which is made only of wheat flour—that they offer almost infinite combinations of texture, flavor, and taste.

Anyone who has traveled across the Asian continent will have seen the rather ramshackle noodle stands along dusty roads in China; bustling noodle bars around Tokyo's busiest railway stations; international bankers slurping noodles while keeping a weary eye on Hong Kong's Hang Seng index, their cellphones tucked into their shoulders; noodle vendors' tiny boats gently paddling through Bangkok's floating markets; Singapore's narrow streets blocked by itinerant food hawkers' plastic tables and chairs; or the tempting smells of noodle-pedlars wafting past sunbathers on the endless beaches of Bali. Noodles are central to Asian food culture.

Choosing noodles

Asian ingredients, once considered strange and difficult to obtain, have become much more widely available, not just from specialty Asian stores but also in supermarkets. Although I have my own reservations about the ever-increasing dependency on supermarkets, I recognize their success in broadening culinary horizons. I can now prepare a gourmet lunch for two in 10 minutes or less.

Wheat Noodles

Wheat noodles are the oldest type of noodle. They were originally from northern China, where the climate is more suited to wheat cultivation, but now are also produced in Japan. As with Italian pasta, some are made with egg in the dough, and others not. Noodles made without egg are always white in color; those made with egg are yellowish. They are made in a variety of shapes and thicknesses, available both dry and fresh.

Cooking instructions are given for dried noodles, and also for fresh, when they are available in that form. The Japanese noodle cooking method deserves special mention (below).

The general rule in choosing the right noodle is to use thinner ones for refined soups, whereas the thicker varieties can stand up to more robust flavors.

Japanese noodle cooking method

All dried Japanese noodles should be cooked in the same way. Bring a saucepan of water to a boil, add the noodles, and return to a boil. Skim off the foam with a slotted spoon, then add a splash of cold water, return to a boil, then skim again. Repeat 2–3 times. When cooked, rinse to remove excess starch, and reheat by dipping in boiling water.

Japanese Udon Noodles

Originating in the Sanuki region of Shikoku Island, udon noodles are made in round, square, or flat shapes. Usually served hot in dashi broth but can also be served stir-fried or chilled. Available fresh in vacuum packs, or in dried form.

Fresh: rinse in warm water and boil for 1 minute

Dried: boil for 3–5 minutes (see method, left)

Japanese Somen Noodles

Udon and soba noodles are seen as the everyday food of the Japanese working man. Somen, on the other hand, are elegant, thin, and white, considered to be more refined and therefore at home in Buddhist temples. They are traditionally served cold with a simple dashi-based dipping sauce. When sold dry, they are often tied with ribbons in neat bundles.

Dried: boil for about 3 minutes (see method, left)

Japanese Ramen Egg Noodles

Ramen noodles are not Japanese, but the Japanese idea of Chinese wheat noodles. They are usually rather crinkled and pale yellow; either fresh or dried. Vacuum-packed Chinese egg noodles make a perfect substitute.

Fresh: rinse in warm water and boil for 2 minutes

Dried: boil for 3–5 minutes (see method, left)

Chinese Wheat Noodles

Often sold in "nests," with one nest making 1 serving.

Fresh: rinse in warm water, boil for 2–3 minutes

Dried: boil for 3–5 minutes

Chinese Thin Yellow Egg Noodles

Fresh: rinse in warm water, boil for 2 minutes

Dried: boil for 3–5 minutes

Chinese Thick Yellow Egg Noodles

Fresh: rinse in warm water, boil for 3 minutes

Dried: boil for 8 minutes

Shanghai Noodles

These noodles can be made from wheat alone, or from a wheat and egg dough. Similar to Japanese ramen.

Fresh: rinse in warm water and boil for 2 minutes

Dried: boil for about 3 minutes (see method, left)

Hokkien Noodles

Thick pale yellow noodles, originally from the Hokkien province of China but nowadays traveling the globe on a Malaysian passport. They are widely used for stir-fry dishes and can be substituted for Shanghai noodles or Peking noodles.

Fresh: rinse in warm water and boil for 2 minutes

Dried: boil for about 3 minutes (see method, left)

Chinese Wonton Wrappers or Skins, and Dumpling Wrappers, Spring Roll Wrappers, Philippine Lumpia Wrappers

Made from wheat and egg noodle dough. Available fresh or frozen in packs of 6–8 oz., usually 3 inches square.

Always fresh or frozen: sold in refrigerator section. If frozen, let thaw. If filling, add filling, seal, then boil for 4–5 minutes, or deep-fry for 1 minute These wrappers are sold in packages of 50–100 in various sizes. Leftover fresh wrappers may be resealed and frozen for future use.

Rice Noodles

In those parts of China and Southeast Asia where wheat isn't grown, rice starch or rice flour is used to make noodles. They are made in thicknesses ranging from the finest hair-thin vermicelli to wide flat ribbons, and are available fresh or dried. Vietnamese rice paper wrappers are also made from rice flour. Used for soups, stir-frying, or deep-frying. They are extremely versatile. If unavailable, bean thread noodles make a good substitute.

Fine Rice Vermicelli Noodles (*banh hoi*)

Fresh: rinse in hot water, then cook for 1 minute

Dried: soak in hot water for 15 minutes and boil for 1 minute or deep-fry for 30 seconds

Thin Rice Vermicelli Noodles (*bun*)

Used in soups and spring rolls. Sold in large packages, or in small bundles of 1 oz. each, suitable for 1 serving.

Fresh: rinse in hot water, then cook for 1 minute

Dried: boil for 1–2 minutes

Rice Ribbon Noodles (*ho fun*)

When fresh, often sold in folded sheets, like a small book. Sometimes uncut, so cut into wide strips before use. Can be used for Vietnamese *pho* noodle soups.

Fresh: rinse in hot water, then cook for 1 minute

Dried: soak in hot (not boiling) water for 15 minutes, then boil for 1 minute, or stir-fry for 1 minute. May also be deep-fried.

Rice Sticks

It can be confusing as Chinese sometimes call rice vermicelli rice sticks. These flat dried noodles made of rice flour and water are available in three main sizes. Thin ones are usually used in soups, while medium, the most popular, are served in soups, stir-fries, and salads. The wider versions are usually used in Thai dishes. Fresh rice sticks are called rice sheet noodles and are sold in either pre-sliced or in whole sheet form.

Fresh: rinse in cold water, then cook for 1 minute

Dried: soak in hot (not boiling) water for 15 minutes, then boil for 1 minute, or stir-fry for 1 minute. May also be deep-fried.

Rice Paper Sheets

Dry, very brittle translucent sheets made of rice flour. Round or triangular in shape, they usually have a patterned surface —the imprint of the bamboo trays on which they are dried.

Always dried: dip into a shallow bowl of warm water until softened (just a few seconds). Put onto a plate or work surface, add filling, then roll up and serve. Do not work on a wood surface, or the sheets will dry out again. Can also be deep-fried until crisp. Sold in packs of 50 large or 100 small. Leftovers may be wrapped in 2 layers of plastic wrap and sealed well.

Bean Thread Noodles

Made from mung bean flour, this family of noodles is also known as cellophane noodles or glass noodles, and include Japanese harusame noodles.

Almost colorless, these dried noodles are sold in bundles of various sizes. For easier handling, I recommend buying smaller sizes, such as the 1 oz. bundles, perfect for 1 serving.

Chinese Bean Thread Noodles

Available in various thicknesses

Dried: soak in hot (not boiling) water for 15 minutes, then drain and boil or stir-fry for 1 minute

Japanese Harusame Noodles

Harusame means "spring rain" in Japanese, and as the name implies, these noodles are thin, delicate, semi-transparent, and white. Traditionally they are used in soups and salads. They have a slightly chewier texture and are interchangeable with shirataki noodles.

Fresh: as for shirataki noodles

Dried: deep-fry until white and puffy, about 30 seconds

Buckwheat Noodles

Usually made from a combination of buckwheat and wheat flour, and sometimes also yam potato starch. They are slightly flecked and usually mushroom colored, they are sold in dried form outside Japan. Elegantly colored green tea noodles (cha-soba) contain ground green tea leaves.

Japanese Soba Noodles

Usually made from a combination of buckwheat and wheat flour, and sometimes also yam potato starch.

They are used in soup or served chilled with dipping sauce. They represent the epitome of noodles in Tokyo, while udons are the noodles of the Osaka region.

Fresh: boil for 2 minutes

Dried: boil for 4 minutes (see method, page 8)

Korean Naeng Myun Noodles

The Korean version of Japanese soba noodles are chewier and paler in color. They are made from a mixture of buckwheat flour, potato starch, and cornstarch. In Korean, the name means "cold noodle," which is the most popular way of serving them. If difficult to find, soba noodles are a good substitute.

Fresh: boil for 3 minutes

Dried: boil for 5 minutes

Potato Starch Noodles

Also made from the starch of the yam potato).

Japanese Shirataki Noodles

Not strictly noodles, but fine strands of *konnyaku*, a jelly-like block made from the starch of a variety of yam, also known as devil's tongue plant. The noodles are often associated with sukiyaki, the Japanese table-cooked dish of beef and vegetables (page 53).

Always fresh: usually sold floating in water in clear, giant, sausage-shaped packages. Harusame noodles are a good substitute.

Korean Dang Myun Noodles

Tougher, stronger, and longer than the Japanese variety, they are resilient and chewy and have the ability to soak up flavors without becoming soggy. Used in jap chae (page 54). If unavailable, bean thread vermicelli noodles make a lighter, less substantial substitute.

Always dried: soak in boiling water for 10 minutes, then drain and stir-fry for 1 minute.

steamed pork noodle dumplings

3 dried shiitake mushrooms

1 lb. ground pork

4 scallions, finely chopped

2 garlic cloves, crushed

1 inch fresh ginger, peeled and grated

½ cup stale bread crumbs

2 tablespoons soy sauce

2 tablespoons hoisin sauce

1 egg, beaten

a small bunch of cilantro, finely chopped

1 lb. fresh thin wheat or egg noodles, or Peking noodles*

1 lb. bok choy, coarsely chopped

Chile Dipping Sauce or Sweet Chile Dipping Sauce (pages 62–63), to serve

a bamboo steamer

Serves 6–8

*If using dried noodles, soak for 5 minutes in hot water, then boil for 1–2 minutes.

Put the shiitake mushrooms in a small bowl, cover with boiling water, and let soak for 10 minutes. Drain. Discard the stems and finely chop the caps.

Put the mushrooms, pork, scallions, garlic, ginger, bread crumbs, soy sauce, hoisin sauce, egg, and cilantro in a large bowl and mix thoroughly. Cover and let stand in the refrigerator for at least 30 minutes to develop the flavors.

Take 1 tablespoon of the mixture and roll between your palms to make a ball. Repeat until all the mixture has been used.

Hold 4–5 strands of noodles in your hand and wrap around the ball, finishing with the noodle ends underneath. Repeat with the remaining balls.

Line a bamboo steaming basket with the bok choy and arrange the wrapped balls, in a single layer, leaving a 1-inch gap between each ball. Cover and set the steamer over a wok or saucepan of simmering water. Steam them for 8–12 minutes or until the dumplings are cooked—the noodles will become glossy when ready.

Transfer the steamed bok choy and dumplings to a platter and serve with a dipping sauce. Alternatively, the dumplings may be served in the steamers.

Variation You may also use thin dried rice noodles—soak them in hot water for 10 minutes before using.

appetizers

sang choy bow
lettuce boat with pork and noodles

2 oz. dried rice vermicelli noodles

3 tablespoons peanut oil

2 garlic cloves, crushed

1 inch fresh ginger, peeled
and finely chopped

8 oz. ground pork and veal,
mixed half and half

4 oz. canned bamboo shoots,
rinsed, drained, and
finely chopped

6 canned water chestnuts,
rinsed, drained, and
finely chopped

1 tablespoon soy sauce

1 tablespoon hoisin sauce

4 scallions, finely chopped, plus
extra to serve

sea salt and freshly
ground black pepper

To serve

16 baby romaine lettuce leaves

2 fresh red chiles, finely chopped
(optional)

Spicy Soy Vinaigrette Dip
(page 63)

Makes 16

This favorite Chinese restaurant dish is easy to make at home. It is usually made with meat only, but extra rice vermicelli noodles will lighten the mixture and give it more texture. I like to use baby romaine lettuce leaves instead of the traditional iceberg lettuce. It's also a very sociable dish—prepare all the elements and let your guests make their own packages.

Put the noodles in a large bowl and cover with boiling water. Let stand for 5 minutes or until the noodles have softened. Drain, rinse under cold running water, and drain as much water you can get out by gently squeezing them with your hand. Cut them into 1-inch lengths with kitchen shears.

Heat the oil in a wok or large skillet and swirl to coat. Add the garlic, ginger, and ground meat and stir-fry over high heat until the meat is well browned, 1–2 minutes.

Reduce the heat to medium and add the bamboo shoots and water chestnuts. Season with soy sauce, hoisin sauce, salt, and pepper.

Turn off the heat, add the noodles and chopped scallions and mix well. (You may prepare up to this point 3 hours in advance.)

Divide the meat mixture into 16 equal portions and spoon each portion into a lettuce leaf. Garnish with chopped scallions. Serve with a dish of chopped red chiles and Spicy Soy Vinaigrette Dip for those who prefer to turn up the heat.

This dish brings back memories of summer evenings when I was a child in Japan. After bathing and changing into a crisp *yukata* (cotton or linen kimono), we would sit on bamboo benches in the garden listening to the chimes of a wind bell and the song of crickets. My grandmother served the white noodles floating in a big lacquered tub of ice water.

chilled somen noodles
with wasabi and dipping sauce

about 1 lb. dried somen noodles (3 oz. per person as an appetizer, 4 oz. as an entrée)

Soy dipping sauce

8 dried shiitake mushrooms

1 cup Dashi (page 62)

½ cup mirin (sweetened Japanese rice wine) or dry sherry

¼ cup soy sauce

To serve

1 inch fresh ginger, peeled and finely grated

1 sheet dried nori seaweed, finely sliced

8 scallions, finely chopped diagonally

1 baby cucumber, peeled and finely sliced

8 cooked shrimp, peeled, but with tail fins intact

Serves 4–6

Put the shiitake mushrooms in a bowl and cover with hot water. Leave to rehydrate for at least 15 minutes or until softened. Drain, reserving the soaking liquid. Cut off and discard the hard stems and thinly slice the caps.

Put the dashi in a saucepan and heat gently until almost boiling. Reduce the heat immediately, add the mirin and soy sauce, and return to a boil. Turn off the heat and let cool to room temperature. You may prepare up to this point the day before and refrigerate until ready to use.

Bring a large saucepan of water to a boil and add the noodles, one bundle at a time. Stir with chopsticks each time you add a bundle to make sure they separate. Watch the saucepan carefully and stand by with a glass of cold water ready.

When the water begins to boil over, add the cold water. This is called *bikkuri mizu* ("surprise water") and it is used to make the outside and inside of the noodles cook at the same speed. Return to a boil and turn off the heat. Drain and rinse the noodles under cold running water, drain again, and chill.

To serve, float the noodles in a large glass bowl or separate small bowls, filled with ice and water. Put the ginger, seaweed, scallions, cucumber, and shrimp onto a separate plate and put the soy dipping sauce in a bowl. Guests choose their own combinations.

lobster noodle salad
with coconut and fruit

An exotic salad I found on vacation in Southeast Asia. Fresh coconuts aren't always available, but if you see them for sale in your market, buy one and try this salad. The type you need is the brown hairy kind.

8 oz. dried bean thread noodles

2 medium-size cooked lobsters

2 fresh coconuts

Dressing

1 tablespoon palm sugar or light brown sugar

freshly squeezed juice of 4 limes

1 teaspoon freshly ground green pepper

1/2 teaspoon salt

2 tablespoons peanut oil

To serve

1 fresh starfruit (carambola), thinly sliced

a bunch of cilantro, coarsely chopped

a bunch of mint leaves, coarsely chopped

2 tablespoons roasted peanuts, coarsely chopped, plus extra to serve (optional)

Serves 4

Put the noodles in a bowl, cover with very hot water, and let soak for 10 minutes or until soft. Drain, rinse under cold running water, and drain again. Chop into 2-inch lengths with kitchen shears and set aside.

Remove the flesh from the cooked lobsters and shred it finely.

Crack open the coconuts and scoop out the white flesh. Using a fork, shred the coconut flesh into small strips.

Put the dressing ingredients in a small bowl and stir well to dissolve the sugar.

Put the noodles in a large bowl, add the lobster and coconut, pour the dressing over the top, and stir gently.

Transfer to a large serving dish, arrange the starfruit slices on top, then add the cilantro, mint, and peanuts. Serve extra peanuts separately, if using.

Useful tip To crack open a coconut, wrap it in a dish towel. Put on a solid base, such as a clean floor, and tap it with a rolling pin.

szechuan bang bang
chicken noodle salad

1 small chicken (about 3 lb.)

1 inch fresh ginger, peeled and grated

1 onion, halved

1 tablespoon salt

8 oz. dried rice vermicelli noodles

8 inches cucumber, peeled and cut into matchstick strips

1 tablespoon pan-toasted sesame seeds, to serve

Chinese sesame dressing

1/3 cup Chinese sesame paste or smooth peanut butter

2 tablespoons sesame oil

2 tablespoons soy sauce

1 tablespoon chile sauce

1 tablespoon sugar

1/2 teaspoon salt

1/4 cup Chicken Stock (page 62)

Serves 4

Put the chicken in a large saucepan, cover with cold water, then add the ginger, onion, and salt. Cover, bring to a boil over medium heat, reduce the heat, and simmer for 45 minutes. Let the chicken cool completely in the stock. This may be done a day in advance.

Remove the chicken and drain well, saving the stock for another use. Skin the chicken, take the meat off the bones, and shred it finely with a fork. Discard the skin and bones.

Put the noodles in a bowl, cover with boiling water, and let soak for 5 minutes. Transfer to a strainer, rinse under cold running water, and drain well. Cut the noodles into 1-inch lengths with kitchen shears and transfer to a serving dish. Spread the cucumber and shredded chicken on top.

Put all the Chinese sesame dressing ingredients in a small bowl, stir well, and pour over the chicken. Sprinkle with the toasted sesame seeds, then serve.

The traditional Bang Bang chicken does not include noodles. However, I have included rice vermicelli to make a refreshing salad or one-dish lunch. If you cook it in advance, you will also have excellent chicken stock as a by-product.

Strict Buddhists are vegetarian, so real shark's fin is out of the question. Substituting rice vermicelli noodles seems more ecologically friendly and hurts no one. You don't have to be a Buddhist to enjoy this light but satisfying soup (though Buddhist monks famously enjoy long, healthy lives).

buddhist "shark's fin" soup

4 oz. dried rice vermicelli noodles

4 dried shiitake mushrooms

4 dried black Chinese mushrooms

4 dried wood ear mushrooms

1 tablespoon peanut oil

½ carrot, cut into matchstick strips

1 leek, thinly sliced

4 oz. canned bamboo shoots, cut into matchstick strips

4 oz. Napa cabbage, thinly shredded

8 oz. bean sprouts, rinsed, drained, and trimmed

3 tablespoons light soy sauce

1 teaspoon sugar

½ teaspoon salt

½ teaspoon sesame oil

2 scallions, finely chopped

1 teaspoon sesame seeds, pan-toasted in a dry skillet

Soak the noodles in boiling water, cover, and set aside for 10 minutes or until the noodles have softened. Drain and cut them into 2-inch lengths with kitchen shears.

Put all the dried mushrooms in a bowl and cover with 1 quart boiling water. Let soak until softened, then drain and keep the juice. Cut off all the stems and discard them. Slice the caps thinly.

Heat a wok over high heat and add the peanut oil. Add the mushrooms, carrot, leek, bamboo shoots, cabbage, and bean sprouts and stir-fry for 5 minutes. Reduce the heat to medium and cook for 5 minutes more. Add the reserved mushroom juice and bring to a boil.

Add the noodles and reduce the heat to low. Season with soy sauce, sugar, and salt. Let simmer for another 5 minutes and turn off the heat.

Ladle into soup bowls, sprinkle with sesame oil, chopped scallions, and sesame seeds, then serve.

Serves 4–6

soups

2 tablespoons peanut oil

8 oz. skinless, boneless chicken thighs, thinly sliced

1 onion, thinly sliced lengthwise

1 leek, split lengthwise, rinsed, well drained, and finely chopped

1 carrot, cut into matchstick strips

8 oz. canned sliced bamboo shoots, rinsed, drained, and cut into matchstick strips

16 snow peas, coarsely chopped

8 oz. bean sprouts, rinsed, drained, and trimmed

1 teaspoon soy sauce

4 dried ramen noodle nests, 3 oz. each

sea salt and freshly ground black pepper

Miso soup

1 quart Chicken Stock (page 62)

1 garlic clove, finely chopped

1 1/2 tablespoons mirin (sweetened Japanese rice wine) or dry sherry

1/4 cup light or medium miso paste

To serve

2 scallions, finely chopped

1 tablespoon Chile Oil (page 62)

1 tablespoon sesame seeds, pan-toasted in a dry skillet

Serves 4

This is a substantial, heartwarming miso soup with a difference from Sapporo, the regional capital of Hokkaido, Japan's northern island. Hokkaido was our equivalent of the "Wild West frontier" in the mid-19th century, when the new government encouraged large numbers of pioneer farmers and miners to go north in search of a new life.
In the harsh and barren winters, non-traditional ingredients such as garlic and chile oil warmed the bodies and hearts of the new settlers.

sapporo miso ramen
with chicken

Heat the peanut oil in a wok and swirl to coat. Add the chicken, onion, leek, carrot, bamboo shoots, snow peas, and bean sprouts and stir-fry over high heat for 5 minutes. Season with the soy sauce, then taste and adjust the seasoning with salt and pepper.

Bring a large saucepan of water to a boil, add the noodles, and cook for 2 minutes. Drain and transfer to 4 deep soup bowls.

Meanwhile, put the stock in a saucepan and bring to a boil. Add the garlic, mirin, and miso paste. Stir thoroughly to dissolve the paste. Ladle the soup over the noodles and top with the stir-fried mixture.

Sprinkle with the scallions, chile oil, and sesame seeds and serve immediately.

In Japanese, *kitsune udon*, means "fox noodles." Evidently, Japanese foxes love deep-fried tofu, *abura age*. Foxes in Japan are revered messengers of the Shinto gods. A pair of stone carvings of foxes stands guard at the entrances to all Shinto shrines. I never thought this story strange until I came to live in England, but cultural differences aside, this is a delicious and comforting noodle dish.

fox noodles

4 sheets *abura age* (deep-fried tofu sheets)

8 fresh shiitake mushrooms, stems removed

4 packages (8 oz. each) vacuum-packed fresh udon noodles

4 scallions, finely chopped

sichimi-tôgarashi (Japanese seven-spice), to serve (optional)

Simmering stock

1 cup Vegetarian Dashi (page 62)

1 tablespoon sugar

½ teaspoon mirin (sweetened Japanese rice wine) or dry sherry

2 teaspoons light soy sauce

Noodle broth

1 quart Vegetarian Dashi (page 62)

1 teaspoon salt

1 tablespoon light soy sauce

2 tablespoons mirin (sweetened Japanese rice wine) or dry sherry

Serves 4

To degrease the deep-fried tofu sheets, put them in a strainer and pour boiling water over them. Turn them over and repeat the process. Cut the tofu sheets into 3 triangles.

To make the simmering stock, put the dashi, sugar, mirin, and soy sauce into a saucepan and heat to simmering over medium heat. Add the tofu triangles and shiitake mushrooms. Simmer for 20 minutes or until the stock has almost disappeared. Turn off the heat and let the tofu cool in the saucepan.

Bring a saucepan of water to a boil and cook the noodles for 2 minutes, stirring them with a pair of chopsticks to separate them. Drain and share between 4 individual bowls.

Put the noodle broth ingredients in a saucepan over medium heat—don't let it boil. When hot, ladle the broth over the noodles in the bowls. Arrange the seasoned tofu triangles on top and top with the shiitake mushrooms and chopped scallions. Serve with a small pot of *sichimi-tôgarashi,* if using.

vietnamese
crab noodle soup

14 oz. dried rice vermicelli noodles

¼ cup Asian dried shrimp

2 tablespoons peanut oil

4 shallots, thinly sliced

2 garlic cloves, crushed

2 fresh red chiles, seeded and finely chopped

4 tomatoes, seeded and coarsely chopped

8 oz. cooked white crabmeat, flaked, fresh, or frozen and thawed

5 cups Chicken Stock (page 62)

2 tablespoons Asian fish sauce

1 teaspoon light brown sugar

1 tablespoon rice vinegar

½ head of iceberg lettuce, thinly sliced

To serve

2 scallions, finely chopped

a handful of cilantro

a handful of mint

1 lime, cut into 4 wedges

Serves 4

This aromatic noodle soup is a speciality of central Vietnam, where all productive land is given over to cultivating rice. The authentic recipe uses tiny freshwater crabs commonly found in paddy fields. Usually they are pounded almost to a paste and made into small dumplings, but this recipe is easier with the crabmeat floating freely in the soup. You don't even have to go crab hunting—I use prepared white crabmeat, fresh or frozen.

Put the noodles in a bowl and cover with boiling water for 10 minutes, or until soft. Drain, rinse under cold running water, and drain again. Using kitchen shears, chop them into manageable lengths, about 2 inches, and set aside.

Put the dried shrimp in another bowl, add ½ cup boiling water, and let soak for 20 minutes. Drain and reserve the shrimp and their soaking water.

Heat the oil in a wok, swirl to coat, then add the shallots, garlic, and chiles. Stir-fry for 1 minute, then add the tomatoes, crabmeat, soaked shrimp, their soaking water, and the chicken stock. Season the soup with fish sauce, sugar, and vinegar and bring to a boil. Reduce the heat to low and let simmer for 5 minutes.

Turn off the heat and stir in the noodles and lettuce.

Ladle the soup into 4 bowls and serve with the scallions, cilantro, mint leaves, and lime wedges on top.

shrimp and spinach
wonton noodle soup

8 oz. fresh or dried egg noodles

1 quart Chicken Stock (page 62)

1 tablespoon soy sauce

4 oz. Chinese greens such as Napa cabbage or bok choy, coarsely chopped

sea salt and freshly ground black pepper

2 scallions, sliced diagonally, to serve

Wontons

2 tablespoons peanut oil

2 oz. spinach, coarsely chopped, about ½ cup

4 oz. uncooked shrimp, peeled, deveined, and finely chopped

1 garlic clove, crushed

1 inch fresh ginger, peeled and finely chopped

6 oz. ground pork

1 egg, separated

20 fresh wonton wrappers

sea salt and freshly ground black pepper

Serves 4

To make the wontons, heat the oil in a wok. Add the spinach and stir-fry over medium heat until soft. Remove from the heat, let cool a little, then squeeze out as much excess juice as possible.

Transfer the spinach to a large bowl, add the shrimp, garlic, ginger, ground pork, egg yolk, salt, and pepper, and mix well.

Put a heaping teaspoon of the pork mixture in the center of a wonton wrapper. Brush the edges of the wrapper with lightly beaten egg white and fold in half to make a triangle.

Wet the two bottom corners of the triangle and seal them together. (You can prepare up to this point 6 hours in advance and keep the wontons covered and refrigerated.)

Bring a large saucepan of water to a boil, add the fresh noodles, if using, and cook for 2–3 minutes. (If using dry noodles, cook for 3–5 minutes). Scoop out the cooked noodles with a strainer and divide among 4 serving bowls—keep the water simmering.

Put the chicken stock in a second saucepan and heat to simmering—try not to boil or the stock will be cloudy. Season with soy sauce, salt, and pepper and keep it simmering.

Return the water to a boil and cook the wontons in batches of 4–5 for 5 minutes each.

Spoon them out and add them to the serving bowls. Using the same boiling water, blanch the Chinese greens for 1 minute, then immediately remove and add to the serving bowls. Ladle the stock into the bowls, top with the scallions, and serve immediately.

This is the Cantonese equivalent of Italian ravioli, though the Chinese would claim that theirs came first. The wonton wrapper is made from egg noodle dough and can be bought fresh or frozen from Asian stores. The size of wrappers and packages varies, but here I have used twenty of the 3-inch size. Any leftover wrappers can be frozen. Surprisingly easy to make, this simple dish sums up the pure yet comforting Cantonese food that is so rarely seen in restaurants nowadays. It is also a good way of getting children to eat spinach.

spicy chicken noodle soup

2 large chicken thighs, about 14 oz.

4 oz. dried bean thread noodles, soaked in boiling water and drained

2 hard-cooked eggs, peeled and halved

4 oz. fresh bean sprouts, rinsed, drained, and trimmed

4 sprigs of cilantro, coarsely chopped

2 tablespoons crisp deep-fried shallots*

Spice paste

2 inches fresh ginger or galangal, peeled and chopped

4 stalks of lemongrass, outer leaves discarded, remainder finely chopped

8 macadamia nuts

10 garlic cloves, crushed

15 small Thai shallots or 3 regular, coarsely chopped

8 kaffir lime leaves, coarsely chopped

1/4 cup peanut oil

2 teaspoons ground turmeric

2 tablespoons ground coriander

Serves 4

*Available in larger supermarkets or Chinese grocers.

To make the spice paste, all ingredients should be chopped or sliced as much as you can before they are processed. Harder ones such as galangal and lemongrass should be processed until smooth, then the softer ingredients added. And whole dried spices should be ground separately from the "wet" spices and added later.

Put the chicken in a saucepan, add 1 quart cold water, and bring to a boil over medium heat. Reduce the heat and simmer for 1 hour. Remove the chicken from the stock and reserve the stock. Skin the chicken, shred flesh with a fork, then discard the skin and bones.

To make the spice paste, put the ginger, lemongrass, and nuts in a blender and work to a smooth paste. Add the garlic, shallots, lime leaves, 2 tablespoons of the peanut oil, the turmeric, and coriander and grind again until smooth.

Heat the remaining 2 tablespoons oil in a wok, add 1/4 cup of the paste (reserving the rest for another use) and stir-fry for 3–4 minutes. Reduce the heat, add the shredded chicken and its stock, and simmer for 20 minutes.

Put the drained noodles in 4 deep bowls, then add the halved boiled eggs and bean sprouts. Gently ladle in the soup mixture. Sprinkle with the chopped cilantro and deep-fried shallots and serve immediately.

Note Any surplus spice paste can be kept refrigerated for 3–4 days or frozen in an ice cube tray.

The people of Taiwan are as passionate about noodles as the people of mainland China. This is an unusual recipe—for some reason, pumpkins are rarely used in noodle dishes in Asia.

stir-fried clams and pumpkin
with rice stick noodles

¼ cup Asian dried shrimp

8 oz. dried rice stick noodles

¼ cup peanut oil

1 lb. fresh clams, cleaned

1 cup Shaohsing (sweetened Chinese rice wine) or dry sherry

1 teaspoon sesame oil

1 garlic clove, finely crushed

1 inch fresh ginger, peeled and finely grated

8 oz. fresh pumpkin, seeded and cut into tiny wedges or strips

1 tablespoon soy sauce

½ teaspoon sugar

sea salt and freshly ground black pepper

4 scallions, finely chopped, to serve

Serves 4

Put the dried shrimp in a bowl, add ½ cup boiling water and let soak for 15 minutes.

Put the noodles in a second bowl, cover with boiling water and let soak for 5–7 minutes. Drain, rinse under cold running water, drain again and set aside.

Heat 3 tablespoons of the oil in a wok and swirl to coat. Add the clams and stir-fry over high heat, tossing frequently. Add the rice wine, cover with a lid and cook for 2–3 minutes, shaking the wok from time to time. Remove all opened clams with a slotted spoon, discard any that are still closed and reserve the cooking juices. Keep the clams warm in a covered bowl.

Heat the sesame oil and the remaining peanut oil in the wok, add the garlic and ginger and stir-fry for 1 minute. Add the pumpkin, cook for 1 minute, then add the shrimp and their soaking water. Add the reserved clam cooking juices and simmer for 5–8 minutes or until the pumpkin is tender.

Add the noodles and toss gently to reheat. Season with soy sauce and sugar, then add salt and pepper to taste.

Serve in heated dishes with the clams and scallions on top.

fish and seafood

A dish using two kinds of Japanese noodles. Buckwheat soba noodles are robust, no-nonsense everyday fare, while harusame are special—as exquisitely fine and delicate as an April shower: in fact their name means "spring rain." If unavailable, use bean thread noodles.

shrimp tempura noodles

8 oz. dried soba noodles

4 oz. dried harusame noodles, cut into 1-inch lengths

12 jumbo shrimp, peeled, deveined, and with shallow cuts made across the belly side

1 quart peanut oil or safflower oil, for deep-frying

Tempura batter

¾ cup ice-cold water

1 egg

1²/₃ cups all-purpose flour, sifted

Dipping sauce

1 cup dashi (page 62)

1 tablespoon mirin (sweetened Japanese rice wine) or dry sherry

1 tablespoon soy sauce

4 oz. daikon (Japanese white radish), finely grated

Serves 4

To make the dipping sauce, put the dashi stock, mirin, and soy sauce in a large bowl, add the grated daikon, and set aside.

Bring a large saucepan of water to a boil, add the soba noodles and stir with chopsticks. Return to a boil. When the water begins to froth, immediately add a cup of cold water. Return to a boil for the third time, then drain and rinse the noodles under cold running water. You may have to repeat this process, depending on how dry the noodles are. Drain well, pile onto 4 dishes, and set aside.

Make the tempura batter just before frying: put the egg and ice-cold water in a bowl, mix well, then sift the flour over the top. Stir briefly then use immediately.

Fill a wok or saucepan one-third full of oil and heat to 375°F, or until a piece of noodle fluffs up immediately. Add all the chopped harusame noodles and cook until they turn white and puff up. Scoop out with a slotted spoon and drain on paper towels. Reheat the oil, dip the shrimp in the batter, and gently slide into the oil. Cook for 2–3 minutes or until the batter turns light golden. Drain well on paper towels.

Put the harusame on top of the soba noodles and top with the shrimp. Serve with the strained dipping sauce.

singapore noodles

8 oz. thin dried egg-noodle nests

2 tablespoons peanut oil

4 shallots, finely chopped

2 garlic cloves, crushed

1 inch fresh ginger, peeled and grated

6 oz. canned water chestnuts, rinsed, drained, and coarsely chopped

8 oz. pork loin, thinly sliced

8 oz. uncooked shrimp, shelled and deveined, but tail fins intact

2 eggs, lightly beaten

2 tablespoons soy sauce

2 tablespoons oyster sauce

2 tablespoons Malay mild curry powder (optional)

sea salt and freshly ground black pepper

To serve

2 scallions, finely chopped

1 tablespoon crisp deep-fried onions*

1/2 cup Chile Dipping Sauce (page 62)

Serves 4

Available in larger supermarkets or Chinese stores.

This is one of those national dishes that is better known outside its country of origin. But it is simple and, above all, versatile—as soon as you understand its basic principle, you can improvise according to whatever you have in your pantry or refrigerator.

Bring a large saucepan of water to a boil, add the egg noodle nests, and cook for 3 minutes, gently stirring with chopsticks to separate the noodles. Do not overcook them because they will be stir-fried later. Rinse in cold running water, drain well, and set aside.

Heat the oil in a wok and swirl to coat. Add the shallots, garlic, and grated ginger and stir-fry for 2 minutes. Add the water chestnuts, pork, and shrimp and stir-fry for 3 minutes more.

Add the beaten eggs and swirl to coat the wok. Cook for 1 minute.

Add the cooked noodles and toss lightly to mix with the other ingredients. Season with soy sauce and oyster sauce. Turn off the heat, stir in the curry powder, if using, then add salt and pepper to taste.

Top with the scallions and crisp deep-fried onions and serve with a separate dish of Chile Dipping Sauce.

burmese **fish curry noodles**

8 oz. dried rice vermicelli noodles

1½ lb. oily white fish cutlets, such as swordfish or yellowtail tuna

2 stalks of lemongrass, bruised

1 inch fresh ginger, cut into 4 slices

2 onions, halved

1 large red chile, such as serrano, halved lengthwise

2 tablespoons fish sauce

3 tablespoons peanut oil

½ Napa cabbage, thinly sliced

3 tablespoons rice flour

2 cups coconut milk

about 1 teaspoon sugar

about 1 teaspoon salt

Curry paste

2 onions, coarsely chopped

4 garlic cloves, crushed

½ inch fresh ginger, peeled and grated

1 stalk of lemongrass, outer leaves discarded, remainder very finely chopped

1 large red chile, such as serrano, seeded and chopped

1 teaspoon shrimp paste

2 teaspoons ground cumin

2 teaspoons ground turmeric

1 teaspoon ground coriander

To serve

lime wedges

deep-fried onions (page 38)

hot red pepper flakes

Serves 4

Even if you know nothing else about Burmese food, you may still be familiar with this dish. Like Burma itself, this robust, aromatic curry draws heavily on the food culture of both India and Southeast Asia. Any leftover curry paste can be frozen in an ice cube tray.

Put the noodles in a bowl, cover with boiling water and let soak for 15 minutes. Drain, then add to a saucepan of boiling water and cook for 1 minute. Drain, and keep the noodles warm.

Put the fish in a saucepan and cover with cold water. Add the lemongrass, ginger, onions, red chile, and fish sauce. Bring to a boil over medium heat, then reduce the heat and simmer for 10 minutes. Remove the fish from the heat and set it aside. Strain the cooking liquid into a bowl and reserve.

To make the curry paste, use a mortar and pestle to pound the onions, garlic, ginger, lemongrass, and chile to a smooth paste. Add the shrimp paste, cumin, turmeric, and ground coriander and mix well.

Heat the oil in a wok and swirl to coat. Add the curry paste and cook for 5 minutes until aromatic.

Add the reserved fish to the wok, then add the cabbage and 1 quart of the reserved fish stock. Bring to a boil, then reduce the heat and simmer for 5 minutes. Put the rice flour in a small bowl, add little water, and stir to dissolve. Add to the curry, then add the coconut milk and stir until thickened. Simmer for 5 minutes, then add sugar and salt to taste.

Put the cooked noodles in a large bowl and ladle the curry on top. Serve with lime wedges, deep-fried onions, and pepper flakes.

Probably the most popular of all the classic Thai stir-fry noodle dishes. It is quick and easy to make, just delicate noodles twisted around plump shrimp and crunchy bean sprouts. It is positively jumping with flavors.

8 oz. dried flat rice stick noodles

¼ cup peanut oil

2 shallots, finely chopped

8 oz. peeled uncooked shrimp, deveined

2 garlic cloves, crushed

2 large eggs, lightly beaten

8 oz. bean sprouts, rinsed, drained, and trimmed

2 tablespoons dried shrimp, ground to powder with a mortar and pestle

Spicy seasoning sauce

2 tablespoons Thai fish sauce

2 tablespoons ketchup

1 tablespoon lime juice

1 tablespoon palm sugar or light brown sugar

To serve

1 tablespoon hot red pepper flakes

2 scallions, finely chopped

2 tablespoons chopped cilantro

1 lime, cut into 4 wedges

Serves 4

pad thai
thai fried noodles

Put the noodles in a bowl, cover with hot water, and let soak for 10–15 minutes until softened. Rinse in cold water, drain well, and set aside.

To make the spicy seasoning sauce, put all the ingredients in a bowl and mix well.

Heat the oil in a wok and swirl to coat. Add the shallots and stir-fry for about 2 minutes or until soft and golden. Add the shrimp and garlic and stir-fry for 3 minutes. Add the egg and cook until softly set, stirring with chopsticks to scramble.

Reduce the heat slightly and add the drained noodles. Add half the bean sprouts and half the ground shrimp and toss well.

Pour the spicy sauce mixture around the edge of the wok and turn off the heat immediately. Stir well to ensure the noodle mixture is well coated with the sauce. Sprinkle with the remaining bean sprouts and ground shrimps, then add the hot red pepper flakes, scallions, and cilantro. Serve in bowls with a lime wedge for squeezing.

marinated duck breast
with soba noodles

2 duck breasts, 8 oz. each

14 oz. dried soba noodles

Marinade

2¾ cups Dashi (page 62)

¼ cup soy sauce

3 tablespoons sake

2 tablespoons mirin (sweetened
Japanese rice wine) or dry sherry

Dipping sauce

1 cup Dashi (page 62)

1 tablespoon soy sauce

1 tablespoon mirin (sweetened
Japanese rice wine) or dry sherry

To serve

2 scallions, finely chopped

2 tablespoons wasabi powder,
dissolved with 1 tablespoon
water into a paste

Serves 4

Trim excess fat from the edges of the duck breasts and prick the skin with a fork.

Heat a skillet over medium heat. Add the breasts skin side down and cook for 8–10 minutes or until the skin is crisp and golden. Drain off the fat. Turn over and cook the other side for 2–3 minutes.

Remove the breasts and plunge them in a bowl of hot water to wash off the fat.

Put the marinade ingredients in a bowl and stir well. Add the cooked breasts and set aside in the refrigerator for at least 3 hours or overnight.

When ready to serve, remove the breasts and cut them into thin slices, about ⅛ inch wide. Mix the dipping sauce ingredients in a small bowl and serve in 4 dipping bowls.

Bring a saucepan of water to a boil, add the soba noodles, and when the water is about to boil over, pour in a cup of cold water and return to a boil. You may have to repeat this once more, depending on how dry the noodles are. Drain and rinse the noodles under cold running water. Drain well again.

Put the noodles on 4 heated plates and arrange the duck slices on top. Sprinkle the chopped scallions over the top and put a small mound of wasabi paste beside them. Serve the dipping sauce separately.

meat and poultry

This is a popular northern Thai curried noodle soup with crisp, deep-fried wheat noodles and is very like the traditional curry noodles of neighboring Burma.

chiang mai chicken noodles

2 cups peanut oil, for deep-frying

1 lb. fresh egg noodles, or 8 oz. dried noodles

2 tablespoons Thai red curry paste

1 teaspoon ground turmeric

1 teaspoon ground cumin

4 boneless chicken thighs, coarsely chopped

1 cup Chicken Stock (page 62)

1 cup canned coconut milk

1 tablespoon Thai fish sauce

4 scallions, finely chopped

1/4 cup coarsely chopped cilantro

To serve

4 pink Thai shallots or 2 regular shallots, thinly sliced

2 limes, halved

1 tablespoon crushed dried red chiles

Serves 4

Put the peanut oil in a wok and heat until a piece of noodle fluffs up immediately. Add half the noodles and deep-fry for 2 minutes or until gold and crisp. Remove, drain on paper towels, and set aside. Drain the oil into a heatproof container and let cool.

Meanwhile bring a saucepan of water to a boil, add the remaining noodles, stir with chopsticks, and cook for 1 minute. Remove, drain, and rinse under cold running water. Drain well and set aside.

Take 2 tablespoons of the reserved oil and heat in the wok. Add the curry paste, turmeric, and cumin and stir-fry for 2 minutes.

Add the chicken and stir-fry for a further 3 minutes. Add the chicken stock and bring to a boil. Reduce the heat, then add the coconut milk and fish sauce. Simmer for 10–15 minutes, then turn off the heat and stir in the scallions and cilantro.

Pour boiling water onto the cooked noodles to reheat; drain, and transfer to 4 large bowls. Ladle the soup over the top, add the deep-fried noodles, and serve with shallots, limes, and dried chiles.

Note. Fresh noodles are best for this recipe, but if unavailable, use dried. Dried noodles take slightly longer to boil and fry.

vietnamese chicken noodle **pho**

1 small chicken (about 3 lb.)
1 tablespoon salt
2 red onions, halved
1 inch fresh ginger, thickly sliced
1 cinnamon stick
1 whole star anise
4 cardamom pods, crushed
2 kaffir lime leaves, coarsely torn
2 teaspoons light brown sugar
1/4 cup fish sauce
8 oz. fresh rice noodles
sea salt and freshly ground black pepper
1/4 cup crisp deep-fried shallots, to serve*

Table salad

8 oz. fresh bean sprouts, rinsed, drained, and trimmed
a handful of fresh mint
a handful of Thai basil
a handful of cilantro
2 scallions, chopped
2 fresh red chiles, finely chopped
1 lime, cut into 4 wedges

Serves 4

Available in larger supermarkets or Chinese stores.

This is a chicken version of the famous Vietnamese beef noodle soup, *pho bo*. Yet it is every bit as full of complex flavors and is as satisfying, but lighter and perhaps more subtle, than the beef version. I prefer to use a whole chicken—you get plenty of superb chicken stock and have cooked chicken left for another meal or two. However, if you are making this dish for only one or two people, use one chicken leg and reduce the quantity of other ingredients accordingly. Whatever the quantity, it is the quality of chicken that is important and determines the flavor of the soup.

Put the chicken in a large saucepan, then add the salt, onions, ginger, cinnamon stick, star anise, cardamom pods, and lime leaves. Add 3 quarts water, bring to a boil over medium heat, and skim off any foam. Reduce the heat to low and let simmer for 3–6 hours. Remove the chicken and pour the stock through a fine strainer into a bowl. Reserve the chicken, keeping it warm in a low oven.

Ladle 1 quart of the stock into a saucepan and season with sugar and fish sauce. Taste and adjust the seasoning with salt and pepper.

Put the rice noodles in a bowl, cover with boiling water, and stir gently with chopsticks to separate. Drain immediately and pour into 4 large soup bowls.

Shred the meat from the chicken thighs and breasts with a fork. Put the shredded chicken on top of the noodles and ladle in the hot soup. Sprinkle with deep-fried shallots.

Serve with a plate of table salad—bean sprouts, herbs, scallions, chiles, and lime wedges for each person to add according to taste.

shanghai pork noodles

1 lb. dried rice vermicelli
or rice stick noodles

4 dried shiitake mushrooms

2 tablespoons dried shrimp

¼ cup peanut oil

1 garlic clove, finely crushed

1 inch fresh ginger,
peeled and grated

2 oz. pork fillet, cut into
matchstick strips

1 carrot, cut into
matchstick strips

2 oz. canned bamboo shoots,
cut into matchstick strips
(or baby corn)

a large handful of snow peas, cut
into matchstick strips

2 tablespoons soy sauce

sea salt and freshly
ground black pepper

2 scallions,
finely chopped, to serve

Serves 4

I have tried so many times to make this recipe more sophisticated, elaborate, and complicated, but no matter what I have tried, it still remains the simplest, easiest, and quickest foolproof stir-fry.

Put the noodles in a large bowl, add boiling water to cover and let soak for 15 minutes. Drain, rinse under cold running water, and drain again.

Put the shiitake mushrooms in a bowl, add ½ cup boiling water, and let soak for 10 minutes. Drain, but keep the soaking water. Remove and discard the stems and slice the caps thinly.

Put the dried shrimp in a bowl, add ½ cup boiling water, and let soak for 10 minutes. Drain, but keep the soaking water.

Heat the oil in a wok and swirl to coat. Add the garlic, ginger, pork, mushrooms, shrimps, carrot, bamboo shoots, and snow peas and stir-fry for 5 minutes or until all are cooked.

Add the noodles and the reserved soaking water from the mushrooms and shrimp. Season with soy sauce, salt, and pepper. Stir well and let the noodles soak up the juices.

Serve in 4 heated bowls and top with chopped scallions.

sukiyaki

1 lb. top-quality sirloin beef, cut into ⅛-inch slices

1 tablespoon sake

1 package fresh shirataki noodles (about 8 oz.), drained

2 large white onions, cut into 8 wedges

8 baby leeks, chopped into 1-inch lengths

8 oz. Chinese greens, such as baby bok choy, shungiku, or mituba, coarsely chopped

8 fresh shiitake mushrooms, stems discarded

1 block firm tofu, well drained and cut into 1-inch cubes

4 fresh eggs, lightly beaten (optional), to serve

1 tablespoon peanut oil, for brushing

Kansai-style wari-shita cooking sauce

1 cup soy sauce

1¼ cups sugar

1 cup mirin (sweetened Japanese rice wine) or dry sherry

a tabletop grill or heavy cast-iron grill pan with separate table burner

Serves 4

This is an easy dish to prepare—the equivalent of Japanese fondue. You arrange all the sliced ingredients on a large platter and you and your guests cook everything at the table—fun for even the most reluctant cook. The traditional dipping sauce is beaten raw egg— I never much cared for it, but I shall leave you to decide.

Arrange the beef slices on a large plate, sprinkle with sake, and set aside. Put the shirataki noodles in a bowl, cover with boiling water, and let soak for 2 minutes. Drain and rinse under cold running water. Drain well, chop coarsely, and add to a serving platter or put in small bowls. Arrange the onion wedges, baby leeks, greens, shiitake mushrooms, and tofu cubes on the platter.

To make the wari-shita cooking sauce, put all the ingredients in a pitcher and stir until the sugar has dissolved. Set aside.

Set the table-top grill on a heatproof surface in the middle of the table, preheat its pan according to the manufacturer's instructions, and seat your guests. Brush the grill pan with the oil, add the onion wedges and baby leeks, and stir-fry for 2 minutes or until soft. Put the beaten eggs, if using, into 4 dipping bowls, one for each guest.

Pour half the cooking sauce in the pan, and when the liquid begins to bubble, add half the remaining vegetables, leaving some space for the beef. Cook 1 beef slice per guest at a time and, as the beef changes color, invite your guests to serve themselves.

Let the guests cook more beef and vegetables themselves. Add more of the cooking sauce to top off the liquid level in the pan.

jap chae korean noodles

8 oz. dried Korean vermicelli noodles (see recipe introduction)

2 dried Chinese black mushrooms

3 tablespoons peanut oil

1 large onion, coarsely chopped

3 garlic cloves, crushed

1 inch fresh ginger, peeled and finely grated

8 oz. sirloin steak, thinly sliced

1 carrot, cut into matchstick strips

1 green bell pepper, seeded and cut into matchstick strips

a bunch of Chinese garlic chives, chopped coarsely

2 teaspoons sugar

1/2 teaspoon salt

2 tablespoons soy sauce

1 teaspoon toasted sesame oil

To serve

2 scallions, finely chopped diagonally

2 tablespoons toasted sesame seeds

Chile Dipping Sauce (page 62)

1 lb. fresh or canned Korean kimchi (optional)

Serves 4

This Korean national dish is eaten for breakfast, lunch, or a one-dish supper—in other words, all the time. Korean vermicelli noodles, made from sweet potato, have a more resilient texture than the Chinese version. If unavailable, use any rice vermicelli or bean thread noodles instead. Serve warm with chile sauce and, of course, the nation's favorite—kimchi, if available.

Bring a saucepan of water to a boil, then add the noodles and stir. Reduce the heat to medium and cook for 3 minutes—do not overcook the noodles. Drain and rinse under cold running water. Drain again and set aside.

Put the mushrooms in a bowl, add 1 cup boiling water, and let soak for 20 minutes or until soft. Drain and slice thinly.

Heat the oil in a wok and swirl to coat. Add the onion and stir-fry over moderate heat for 3 minutes. Add the garlic, ginger, and steak and stir-fry for 2 minutes more.

Add the carrot, green bell pepper, mushrooms, and Chinese garlic chives and stir-fry for 2 minutes. Turn off the heat. Season with sugar, salt, soy sauce, and sesame oil and mix well. Turn the heat back on for 1 minute, fold in the noodles, and stir gently.

Ladle into 4 dishes and top with scallions and sesame seeds. Serve with Chile Dipping Sauce, and a bowl of kimchi, if using.

10 oz. dried Korean naeng myun noodles or Japanese soba noodles

1 tablespoon sesame oil

8 oz. daikon (Japanese white radish), peeled and finely grated

1 teaspoon ground chiles

2 tablespoons rice vinegar or cider vinegar

1 teaspoon sugar

1/2 teaspoon salt

2 baby cucumbers, peeled and cut into 2-inch matchstick strips

1 crisp Japanese nashi pear or other firm pear, peeled and cut into 2-inch matchstick strips

Seasoning paste

4 garlic cloves, crushed

2 tablespoons hot chile paste

2 tablespoons sugar

2 teaspoons sesame oil

1 tablespoon sesame seeds, toasted in a dry skillet

Spicy beef

2 tablespoons peanut oil

2 garlic cloves, well crushed

1 lb. sirloin steak, sliced into thin strips

2 tablespoons soy sauce

1 tablespoon sugar

2 scallions, finely chopped

1/2 teaspoon ground black pepper

1–2 tablespoons chile paste

Serves 4

korean beef
with cold buckwheat noodles

Naeng myun means "cold noodle"—indeed, my first encounter with this dish was on a hot summer's day in Seoul. I was quite revived by its punchy flavors and amazing combinations of crunchy textures. Naeng myun are Korea's answer to soba noodles, but are chewier and have a lighter, more translucent appearance. The dried variety can be found in Korean or some other Asian stores, but soba noodles can be used instead.

Bring a large saucepan of water to a boil, add the noodles, and cook until the foam begins to rise. Add a cup of cold water and let the water return to a boil (you may have to repeat this until the noodles are cooked *al dente*). Stir with chopsticks to separate. Drain and rinse in cold water to remove the starch, then drain again. Stir in the sesame oil to stop the noodles from sticking together, then cover and refrigerate.

To prepare the beef, heat the oil in a wok, add all the ingredients for the spicy beef, and stir-fry for 3 minutes. Set aside.

Put the grated daikon in a bowl and stir in the ground chiles, vinegar, and sugar. Set aside.

Sprinkle salt onto the cucumber strips and leave for 10 minutes. Drain and pat them dry with paper towels.

Put all the seasoning paste ingredients in a bowl and mix well.

Put the noodles, daikon mixture, cucumbers, pear, and beef in a large bowl and toss well. Serve with a dish of seasoning paste.

No matter how often I make this dish, each time I still get a childish excitement when the fine vermicelli noodles puff up in the oil and turn into a beautiful sculpture. It makes you feel like a wizard in the kitchen. You may vary the ingredients according to taste and season. Spectacular and deliciously crunchy.

thai mee krob
with stir-fried pork and chicken

1 quart peanut oil, for deep-frying

4 oz. thin dried rice vermicelli noodles

6 shallots, thinly sliced

2 garlic cloves, finely crushed

1 large fresh red chile, seeded and finely chopped

10 oz. ground chicken

6 oz. uncooked peeled shrimp, finely chopped

4 oz. fresh bean sprouts, rinsed, drained, and trimmed

2 tablespoons palm sugar or light brown sugar

2 tablespoons Thai fish sauce

2 tablespoons rice vinegar

freshly squeezed juice of 1 lime

To serve

1–2 fresh red chiles, finely chopped

¼ cup coarsely chopped cilantro

4 scallions, chopped

Serves 4

Fill a wok or deep-fat fryer one-third full of oil, or to the manufacturer's recommended level. Heat the to oil 350°F or until a piece of noodle fluffs up immediately. Cut the noodles into short, manageable lengths with kitchen shears. Cook a small bundle of noodles at a time—they take only a matter of seconds to puff up and turn golden, so if you cook them a few at a time, they won't be overcooked.

As each bundle is cooked, remove and drain on paper towels. Keep them warm in a low oven while you cook the remainder.

Heat 1 tablespoon of the oil in a second wok, add the shallots, and stir-fry for 2–3 minutes. Add the garlic, chile, chicken, shrimp, and bean sprouts and toss for 3 minutes more.

Reduce the heat and season with sugar, fish sauce, and vinegar and mix well. Turn off the heat and add the lime juice.

Put two-thirds of the noodles onto a large heated serving dish. Add the cooked mixture, then the chopped chiles, cilantro, and scallions and top with the remainder of the noodles and serve. Alternatively, serve on 4 separate plates.

pancit canton

8 oz. thick dried egg noodles

1 tablespoon sesame oil

¼ cup peanut oil

1 onion, thinly sliced

2 garlic cloves, finely crushed

4 oz. bacon, finely chopped

8 oz. Napa cabbage, thinly sliced

1 carrot, cut into matchstick strips

1 celery stalk, cut into
matchstick strips

4 oz. fresh bean sprouts,
rinsed, drained, and trimmed

½ teaspoon salt

1 teaspoon sugar

1 tablespoon soy sauce,
plus extra to serve

1 tablespoon oyster sauce

a pinch of freshly ground pepper

1 cup Chicken Stock (page 62)

chile sauce, to serve

Serves 4

Pancit Canton simply means "Chinese noodles" in the Philippines. My children were brought up on this dish whenever I was off duty in the kitchen. It is simple—just a Filipino adaptation of chow mein. You may, and should, improvise with whatever you can find in your refrigerator.

Bring a large saucepan of water to a boil, add the noodles and cook for 2 minutes, gently stirring with chopsticks to separate them.

Drain, rinse under cold running water and drain again. Transfer to a bowl, sprinkle with the sesame oil and stir briefly to keep the noodles separate. Set aside.

Heat 2 tablespoons of the peanut oil in a wok, add the onion, garlic, bacon, cabbage, carrot, celery and bean sprouts and stir-fry for 3–5 minutes.

Season the mixture with salt, sugar, soy sauce, oyster sauce and pepper. Transfer the mixture to a bowl and set aside. Wipe the wok clean with paper towels.

Heat the remaining oil in the wok, add the noodles, toss for 1 minute, then add the chicken stock. Bring to a boil. and when the liquid is reduced to about half, add the stir-fry mixture and mix well for 2 minutes. Taste and adjust the seasoning with soy sauce, salt and pepper.

Serve in 4 heated dishes, with extra soy sauce or chile sauce served separately.

sauces and stocks

sweet chile dipping sauce

Sweeter, less salty, and less sharp than chile dipping sauce.

8 oz. fresh chiles, seeded

4 garlic cloves, crushed

1 teaspoon salt

½ cup brown sugar

½ cup water

Put the chiles in a saucepan, add ½ cup water and cook until soft. Blend with the remaining ingredients, then return to the saucepan and cook over low heat for 10–15 minutes. Let cool, then store in an airtight container in the refrigerator. It will keep for 4 weeks.

nuóc cham dipping sauce

The classic Vietnamese dipping sauce. Vegetarians use light soy sauce instead of fish sauce. It must be used the day it's made.

1 tablespoon sugar

1 teaspoon rice vinegar

1 red bird's eye chile, chopped

2 garlic cloves, finely crushed

1 tablespoon lime juice

2 tablespoons fish sauce

Heat ¼ cup water in a small saucepan, add the sugar and vinegar, and stir to dissolve the sugar. Let cool, then add the remaining ingredients.

spicy soy vinaigrette dip

A dipping sauce with more depth and flavor than soy and rice vinegar. Good with deep-fried dishes.

½ cup soy sauce

1 tablespoon Chile Dipping Sauce

freshly squeezed juice of 1 lime or ½ lemon

2 tablespoons rice vinegar

Mix all the ingredients in a screw-top jar and shake well. Keeps in the refrigerator for up to 1 week.

asian pesto

Toss through any plain fresh hot noodles, just like an Italian pesto. It doesn't keep, so use immediately to capture the fresh herbal flavors.

2 oz. roasted unsalted peanuts

3 cups coarsely chopped cilantro, including some stems

½ cup coarsely chopped Thai or sweet basil

½ cup coarsely chopped mint

4 scallions, coarsely chopped including green parts

grated zest and juice of 2 unwaxed limes

⅓ cup canned coconut milk

1 large green chile, seeded

1 large garlic clove, crushed

1 teaspoon sugar

1 teaspoon salt

1 teaspoon freshly ground green or white pepper

Put all the ingredients in a blender or food processor and grind to a smooth paste.

dashi

Dashi is the basic Japanese stock. Quick and easy to make, it appears in almost every aspect of Japanese cooking.

postcard-size piece of konbu (dried kelp)

1 oz. dried bonito fish flakes

Wipe the konbu with a damp cloth. Put in a saucepan and add 1 quart cold water. Bring to a boil over medium heat and remove the konbu just before the water starts to boil. Let the water boil for a minute, then turn off the heat. Add the bonito flakes and let them settle to the bottom.

Strain the stock through a strainer lined with cheesecloth. Dashi does not keep, so use it the same day.

For vegetarian dashi, omit the bonito and double the quantity of konbu.

chicken stock

2 lb. chicken bones, necks and wings

1 onion, unpeeled and halved

1 inch fresh ginger, thickly sliced

2 garlic cloves, crushed

1 teaspoon salt

Wash the chicken bones and put in a large heavy saucepan. Add the other ingredients and cover with 2–3 quarts cold water. Bring to a boil over medium heat. Skim off the foam. Reduce the heat and simmer for 3 hours. Let cool, then pour through a fine-meshed strainer. The stock can be refrigerated for 5 days or frozen in ice cube trays.

chile oil

I prefer to make my own chile oil—the flavor is better than store-bought ones and it is much more economical. A few drops go a long way. It will keep almost indefinitely in a screw-top bottle stored in a cool, dark place.

1 cup peanut oil

¼ cup sesame oil

¼ cup crushed hot red pepper

1 teaspoon black peppercorns

Heat both oils in a wok over high heat until almost smoking. Add the pepper flakes and peppercorns. Remove from the heat and let cool. Pour through a fine strainer and store in a screw-top bottle.

chile dipping sauce

The level of heat of this dipping sauce depends on the chiles you choose. I use large ones, with a heat level that's easier to control than the small Thai varieties.

8 oz. fresh red chiles, seeded

4 garlic cloves, crushed

2 tablespoons coarsely chopped fresh ginger

¼ cup soy sauce

2 tablespoons sugar

1 teaspoon salt

⅔ cup rice vinegar

Put the chiles in a saucepan and cover with water. Cook over medium heat until soft. Drain and transfer to a blender. Add all the other ingredients and blend to a smooth paste. Transfer the mixture back to the saucepan and cook over low heat for 10–15 minutes. Let cool, then store in an airtight container in the refrigerator. It will keep for 4 weeks.

index

conversion charts

Weights and measures have been rounded up or down slightly to make measuring easier.

VOLUME EQUIVALENTS:

American	Metric	Imperial
1 teaspoon	5 ml	
1 tablespoon	15 ml	
¼ cup	60 ml	2 fl.oz.
⅓ cup	75 ml	2½ fl.oz.
½ cup	125 ml	4 fl.oz.
⅔ cup	150 ml	5 fl.oz. (¼ pint)
¾ cup	175 ml	6 fl.oz.
1 cup	250 ml	8 fl.oz.

WEIGHT EQUIVALENTS:

Imperial	Metric
1 oz.	25 g
2 oz.	50 g
3 oz.	75 g
4 oz.	125 g
5 oz.	150 g
6 oz.	175 g
7 oz.	200 g
8 oz. (½ lb.)	250 g
9 oz.	275 g
10 oz.	300 g
11 oz.	325 g
12 oz.	375 g
13 oz.	400 g
14 oz.	425 g
15 oz.	475 g
16 oz. (1 lb.)	500 g
2 1b.	1 kg

MEASUREMENTS:

Inches	Cm
¼ inch	5 mm
½ inch	1 cm
¾ inch	1.5 cm
1 inch	2.5 cm
2 inches	5 cm
3 inches	7 cm
4 inches	10 cm
5 inches	12 cm
6 inches	15 cm
7 inches	18 cm
8 inches	20 cm
9 inches	23 cm
10 inches	25 cm
11 inches	28 cm
12 inches	30 cm

OVEN TEMPERATURES:

110°C	(225°F)	Gas ¼
120°C	(250°F)	Gas ½
140°C	(275°F)	Gas 1
150°C	(300°F)	Gas 2
160°C	(325°F)	Gas 3
180°C	(350°F)	Gas 4
190°C	(375°F)	Gas 5
200°C	(400°F)	Gas 6
220°C	(425°F)	Gas 7
230°C	(450°F)	Gas 8
240°C	(475°F)	Gas 9